Tank Tactics

Tank Tactics

by
Kenneth Macksey

with illustrations by
Allard Design Group

ALMARK

Almark Publishing Co Ltd London

First Published 1976.

ISBN 85524 250 7

Distributed in the U. S. A. by
Squadron/Signal Publications Inc.,
3461 East Ten Mile Road,
Warren, Michigan 48091.

Printed in Great Britain by
Edwin Snell Printers,
Park Road, Yeovil,
Somerset.
for the publishers, Almark Publishing Co. Ltd.
49 Malden Way, New Malden,
Surrey KT3 6EA, England.

Contents

Introduction to the Mechanics of War

Tank Tactics by Kenneth Macksey introduces The Mechanics of War, a new series from Almark.

The first four books cover the tactics employed by the three land and the air arms during the Second World War in Europe.

Shelford Bidwell writes on Artillery, Anthony Farrar-Hockley on Infantry, and Christopher Chant on Ground Attack.

They cover the neglected area of small unit tactics which are the basis of every great battle and explain how company, squadron or battery orders were passed down and carried out. The books give the reader an insight into how the historic strategic decisions of the war became the tactics of the soldier on the ground.

The Mechanics of War will follow these books with a nation by nation coverage of the uniforms, small arms, tanks and artillery used in Europe, the Mediterranean and Russia.

Each volume will show how a nation used and modified its weapons and equipment in the light of tactical experience in each campaign.

Acknowledgements

All pictures with the exception of those listed below are from the Imperial War Museum collection. Pages 32, 69, British Official. Page 63 Almark. Page 46 Novosti. Diagrams Pages 9, 21, 29, 37, 45, 50, 61 Michael Haine.

Birth of the Blitzkrieg

The tank organisations and tactical procedures of the Second World War did not appear beautifully fashioned without passing through several arduous stages of development. They came into existence through an evolutionary process moulded by battle, the demands of the soldiers for more sophisticated fighting machines than the original tanks of 1915, the restrictions imposed by financial, material and industrial restraints and the influence exerted by the geographical and political aims of the leading nations.

Battle's exigencies sired the tank for soldiers who were penned in trenches by barbed wire and intensive artillery and machine-gun fire, and for whom, to move above ground level, was almost suicidal — even when immense artillery fire support was expended in their aid. The initial concept of the tank was as a device to cross broken ground in order to roll down gaps through barbed wire barriers and apply accurate direct gun-fire against enemy machine-guns and artillery emplacements. To get to close enough quarters for that the machine had to be armoured against as many types of enemy fire as possible, although it was realised by early 1917 that a fighting vehicle proof against field artillery fire would weigh 100 tons, and this would place an unacceptable load on industrial and financial resources. And so the first concession to non-battlefield constraints was made. Tanks that were vulnerable would have to be accepted

into service and would be compelled to compensate for that vulnerability by greater speed and manoeuvrability, by superior hitting power to that of the enemy, and through subtly designed tactical procedures allied with co-operation with all the other elements to be found on a battlefield — above all with artillery, engineers and infantry.

The original tank tactics of breaching a trench line in 1917 were carefully pre-planned prior to each action and reduced to a simple drill: there was no other way because there was no intercommunication between tanks and the supporting arms. Tanks advanced in two waves, the first, unaccompanied, to flatten wire, fill anti-tank ditches with fascines (great bundles of wood carried by the tank) and generally to dominate the enemy defences, while the second, with infantry in attendance, entered and cleared the fortifications. To perform these multiple functions the British built large 30 ton tanks that carried both cannon and machine-guns. A little later the French produced tanks that were, in effect, armoured assault guns whose task was mainly to give direct cannon fire support to the advancing infantry. In due course they also produced light tanks of about 7 tons with a single machine-gun in a one man turret — an armoured machine-gun carrier, in fact. But not until 1918 was a serious proposition to project the tank attack beyond the immediate front battle zone considered. That year Colonel J. F. C.

Left: Sherman tanks with their British crews massed at a concentration area in France in 1944. In the background is a Scammell 6×4 Heavy Breakdown Tractor. Of interest are the rimless paratrooper type helmets on the turrets of the tanks. These helmets were less restrictive than the standard infantry helmet when worn in the cramped interior of a tank.

Fuller, the chief staff officer of the British Tank Corps, submitted a scheme to capitalise on the advent of the latest type of fast, manoeuverable tank with its circuit of action up to 100 miles. He envisaged these 'medium' machines (weight about 20 tons) breaking through the front in conjunction with the by then conventional, breaching operation by infantry support tanks, to strike swiftly and deeply into the enemy communication zone and cause command and logistical disruption. With the medium tanks would go infantry in lorries and motorised artillery while aircraft helped by bombing enemy headquarters and artillery positions. Drafted as the basis for the campaign in 1919 (and called Plan 1919) it was stillborn when the war ended in November 1918. Basically, however, these two methods laid the foundation of all future tank tactics.

Nevertheless the only proven kind of tank tactics that survived as standard practice in the post war years were those of direct infantry support: Fuller's proposals for deep strategic penetration stayed locked in the realms of conjecture, awaiting the advent of enough machines of the required specification to prove his idea's feasibility. The design in 1922 by Vickers Ltd of what became known as the Medium Tank produced just such a machine — one with the desired range, speed and

Light tanks (Mk VIb) head a column of British medium tanks during a pre-war exercise on Salisbury Plain. It was during these exercises that the British learned lessons in tank warfare that they neglected during the first years of the war.

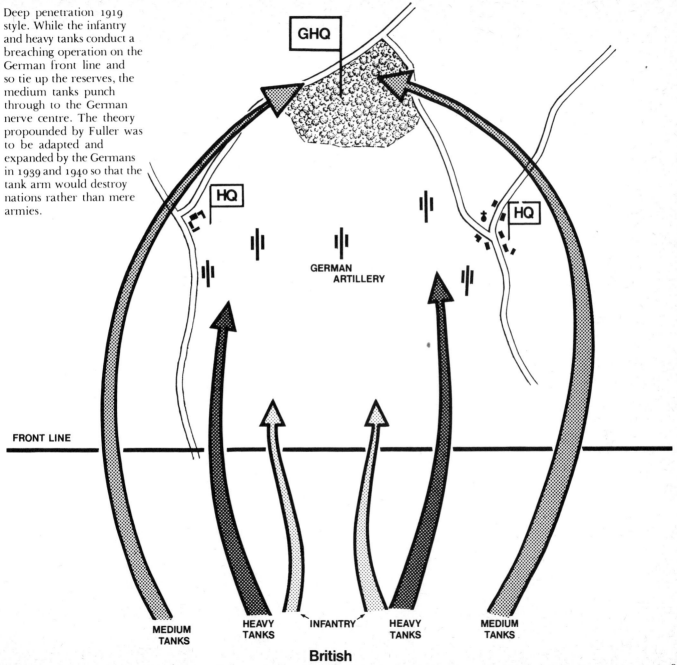

Deep penetration 1919 style. While the infantry and heavy tanks conduct a breaching operation on the German front line and so tie up the reserves, the medium tanks punch through to the German nerve centre. The theory propounded by Fuller was to be adapted and expanded by the Germans in 1939 and 1940 so that the tank arm would destroy nations rather than mere armies.

GHQ

HQ

HQ

GERMAN
ARTILLERY

FRONT LINE

MEDIUM
TANKS

HEAVY
TANKS

INFANTRY

HEAVY
TANKS

MEDIUM
TANKS

British

Right: Dummy tanks used by the German Army for training. Due to the Versailles Treaty restrictions the Germans were forbidden to use armoured vehicles, but these cars with plywood or cardboard "armour" gave them a grounding in tank tactics. '

Far Right: A Russian T 35 knocked out in 1941. The multi-turreted tank was conceived as a sort of land battleship. All the major powers experimented with them in the 1920s and '30s, but they were slow and vulnerable.

A British tank crew prepare a shelter against the side of their Mk VI during the early days of the war in North Africa.

durability in action. Its acceptance into production did more than create a pilot model for the future — a tank with a fully rotating turret that housed both the main armament (a gun of high velocity with a good anti-armour capability) and a three man turret crew consisting of commander, gunner and loader/radio operator. Using this tank, supported by light tanks for reconnaissance and protection purposes, cross-country lorries for infantry and mechanised artillery in support, the British were able to experiment tactically throughout the 1920s and early 1930s and to demonstrate that mechanised forces, based upon the tank, could function efficiently

and with dominating effect in most of the main operations of war, even in quite difficult country. But both they and the French continued to give priority to the original concept of direct infantry support actions, and they were copied by the other armies of the world, including those of Russia and the USA.

In Germany, too, there was a majority in favour of direct infantry support, but the Treaty of Versailles denied Germany tanks (except for a few clandestinely produced models) until 1934 and so, for the most part, ideas alone could be developed. But those ideas were seized upon by a brilliant and dynamic innovator who was convinced that

Fuller was right. Oberst Heinz Guderian, by building upon Fuller's proposals and copying British organisations and tactics, evolved the German *panzertruppe* and, eventually, the first genuine all-arms mechanised formations — the panzer divisions — with their integrated tank, infantry, artillery, engineer and administrative units. Moreover it was Guderian and his apostles who, by adapting the existing German practice of *ad hoc* battle groups to include tanks as well as infantry and light assault artillery, created the flexibly powerful combat teams that enabled groups, founded upon the tank, to exploit their full potential. As the rock upon which such a flexible scheme had

Above: A *Panzerbefehlswagen* III or armoured command vehicle on a Mk III tank chassis. This tank had provision for extra radios and carried a dummy gun to give space for the radios and crew.

Above Right: A *Kleiner Pänzerbefehlswagen* I. This had a fixed turret, a crew of three and extra radio.

to be built, however, was a modern system of command and control, with personal leadership by senior commanders who mostly passed their orders by radio to tanks and support vehicles which, in return, could supply a flow of quick information about a fast developing situation from the forefront of combat. Everything was dependent upon swift and reliable communications for the fastest possible execution of orders so that a shaken enemy was denied recovery of his composure.

There were two important originations in German tactical techniques. In the first place Guderian realised that a tank's speed gave something more than added protection against fire by making it a more difficult target to hit. He understood that a tank formation's speed of advance in space gave it protection against total enemy reaction. If a moving force was difficult to locate and pin down, concentration against it was difficult. Hence enemy attacks were likely to arrive piecemeal and might often hit thin air. Secondly, while

conceding that there would be occasions upon which a direct assault upon the enemy would become unavoidable, with attendant losses to tanks, he aimed to minimise his own losses during *offensive* operations by fighting as often as possible from a *defensive* posture. The technique was simple. Air and ground reconnaissance units (the latter comprising armoured cars and motor-cycle mounted infantry) located the gaps or thinly held sectors in the enemy line. Armoured all-arms battle groups broke through rapidly by surprise and raced for the vital ground in the enemy rear with the tanks leading, their route very often directed through the most difficult, and therefore least heavily defended, terrain. Having reached the objective, a defensive 'hedgehog', composed of anti-tank guns protected by infantry and tanks, was established and the enemy provoked into attacking this at a disadvantage. A series of linked local operations such as these could bring about a total disruption of the enemy defences. It was, in essence, an extemporisation of the attack upon weakness such as the Germans had evolved in 1917 for infantry and cavalry. Its ultimate aim was the total encirclement of the enemy by a threat or movement upon his flank and rear — be it at

Russian soldiers receive instruction on the engine of a T 60 light tank.

Below: A Russian troop commander briefs his men. Behind them is a T 34/76D, probably the commander's tank.

the highest strategic level, involving Army Groups, or the lowest involving companies and sections.

The Russians, who built many thousands of tanks in the 1930s, tried to copy the Germans and so, with meagre resources, did the Americans. But the experience of the Spanish Civil War between 1936 and 1939 seemed to suggest that the concept of the deep penetration scheme was defective. Tanks that raced about on their own had been usually destroyed by anti-tank guns. That the essential co-operation between all arms that Guderian advocated had been missing (due to lack of good communications) was overlooked, and it was only by the superhuman efforts of the German enthusiasts that the panzer divisions were saved from being broken up, as with other armies, among the infantry. When war broke out in 1939 only the Germans possessed fully formed armoured divisions since, although the French had a few formations which were panzer divisions in outline, they were not so in tactical doctrine; and Britain's two partially equipped armoured divisions were not ready. In practice the employment of French and British armoured formations was different from that of the Germans. While the Germans tended to stand-off in

The crews of a troop of Sd Kfz 231 heavy armoured cars are briefed on the Western Front in 1940. The Germans used their armoured cars to seek out weak spots in the enemy lines which could be exploited by tanks.

concentrations and employ their guns at maximum range to destroy the enemy, the French either used their tanks in the traditional role of cavalry reconnaissance, spread across the front, or sought to arrive at close quarters by charging to the mouth of the guns — and the British did much the same. As a result they both played into the hands of the Germans and either sacrificed themselves in 'penny packets' or committed a Balaclava-like suicide against emplaced German guns.

Action at the front, the manoeuvring of machines and the direction of fire, are the obvious manifestations of tactics but are impossible if an adequate supply of fuel and ammunition cannot be made available. While

Polish, French and British supply systems fell apart, it was a touchstone of the German system that the superb logistical organisation they had created never deprived the fighting troops of supplies in 1939 and 1940, and only failed thereafter because the German nation and its armed forces took on more than they could handle. The supply organisation for fast moving armoured forces had need, of course, to be tactically regulated because the truck columns had often to move deep into enemy territory. Self-protection as often the order of the day both for convoys and the small depots that were set up near communication centres. Sometimes when enemy counter-thrusts threatened the supply routes and depots,

A PzKw 38(t) is loaded onto a Me 323 "Gigant" transport aircraft. The 38(t) was a Czech tank. Many were captured by the Germans and used in France and Poland.

armoured forces had to be diverted for their protection. Indeed, since armoured thrusts were often aimed initially against the heart and arteries of enemy supply, and effective counter moves were often profitable by the enemy against the sources of the attacking armoured forces, contending strategic plans frequently resolved themselves into struggles for possession or destruction of the logistic organisations.

Throughout the war variations on the German theme were played with abandon and ever increasing violence. Their concept of all-arms operation predominated and was enthusiastically copied and developed by their enemies. Nevertheless the demands of

economy conditioned policy. Short of material and manpower, the Germans were compelled to concentrate their resources and hence starved their purely infantry formations of armoured support. Yet gradually they were compelled to introduce special infantry support units comprising either assault guns or the very expensive and relatively uncommon heavy tanks that began gradually to appear as the war progressed (see below).

Blessed, as they were, with almost unlimited resources, the British, Russians and Americans could afford two separate kinds of tank organisation; formations of medium tanks for the armoured divisions (the Russians, for example equipped their Tank Groups,

The crew of a T 34/76 medium tank. The T 34 was one of the best tanks of the war, and though lacking many of the fittings of western tanks its simplicity made mass production easier.

Below: Russian soldiers bunch round a T 34 during fighting in the winter of 1941-42. In the early days of the war the Russian tactics were rigid and predictable and negated the advantages of many of their weapons.

Dalshey Poddierzhki with the T 34 tank and its 76mm gun in a fully rotating turret), and of heavy or medium tanks in special Infantry Tank Brigades for close infantry support (to quote the British example which finally used the Churchill tank with a 75mm gun in this role).

But while the basic pattern of armoured operations changed but little, alterations in detail were caused universally by the rapid increase in the size, weight, protective and hitting power of AFVs that were brought into service in attempts to extend the influence of armour while warding off the ever increasing threat of anti-armour weapons. For example, the frontal armour thickness of main battle tanks in 1940 varied between 30 and 60mm, but by 1942 nothing less than 80mm was acceptable. And whereas the largest anti-tank gun in general service in 1940 was 47mm, by 1943 anything under 75mm was considered inadequate. In consequence tank weights rose from about 25 or 30 tons to the 40 — 50 ton mark in 1943 — with some even larger than that.

Apart from the crucial need to retain at least a semblance of technical parity, if not superiority, over the enemy, armoured leaders had always to nurture the morale of their crews which tended to oscillate in relation to the battlefield effectiveness of their equipment. To know that the enemy had a capacity to penetrate defensive armour at normal battlefield ranges (usually between 800 and 1,200 metres) and yet realise ones' own inability to retaliate, could destroy a tank crew's confidence and deter it from seeking battle. But for a crew to be aware of its invulnerability and capability of destroying the enemy at minimum risk was mighty encouraging to aggressive intentions. The Germans had feelings of superiority until they found themselves outmatched technically by the Russian T 34s and KV Is late in 1941, and they restored their morale by introducing modified machines in 1942. Likewise the superior German Panther and Tiger tanks heavily eroded the confidence of American and British Sherman and Cromwell tank crews in 1944.

The need to mount a gun that was big enough and of high enough velocity to both shell the enemy with high explosive *and* penetrate his thickest armour at long ranges, placed fresh demands upon vehicle designers. While it was generally recognised that the orthodox tank with its fully rotating turret was ideal and wholly desirable, a use could also be found for a cheaper, more easily manufac-

tured AFV in which the gun was carried in the hull, pointing forwards, and given only a limited traverse. This was a reversion to the original French idea of assault artillery, and imposed tactical constraints of its own. For an AFV of this sort was at a grave disadvantage in the forefront of an attack since its flank protection was weak, its tactical characteristics were best suited to support from lay-back positions in the assault and, primarily, as a mobile anti-tank gun within a static defensive locality.

A crew man of a KV I re-arms his tank with drums of machine gun ammunition and shells for the 76.2- mm gun. The chassis was the basis for a number of variations of assault guns and tanks.

A Sherman Firefly negotiates a partially demolished bridge south of Bentivoglio in Italy. The Firefly was armed with a 17-pounder gun which had superior penetrating power to the standard 75-mm gun.

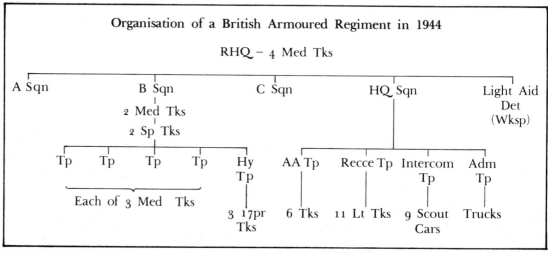

Organisation of a British Armoured Regiment in 1944

RHQ – 4 Med Tks

A Sqn   B Sqn   C Sqn   HQ Sqn   Light Aid
                                                             Det
               2 Med Tks   (Wksp)
               2 Sp Tks

     Tp   Tp   Tp   Tp   Hy   AA Tp   Recce Tp   Intercom   Adm
                         Tp   Tp   Tp

     Each of 3 Med Tks   6 Tks   11 Lt Tks 9 Scout   Trucks
                         3 17pr   Cars
                         Tks

The British Experience

In 1944 the preparations for battle and the style of combat had become virtually standardised within an ordinary tank regiment. To describe one nation's methods is to relate the procedure of another. On the eve of the invasion by the Allied armies of Normandy in June, a British armoured regiment such as formed part of an armoured division was organised as shown opposite.

Its main striking power added up to 61 Sherman medium tanks (they were sometimes Cromwells, but both were similarly armed with one 75mm and 2 machine-guns, though gradually a few tanks with the 76.2mm, 17 pdr gun were being introduced to Shermans called Fireflies) and 11 light tanks (Stuarts with a 37mm gun as main armament) to act in reconnaissance. In support of these 72 fighting vehicles were scout cars, recovery vehicles and a fleet of trucks manned by a total of 666 officers and men. It was, therefore, a highly mobile, self-contained organisation that could move fast and far across country on its tracked or four-wheeled drive vehicles and be capable of delivering a heavy weight of accurately aimed fire-power while the crews of its armoured vehicles — the tanks — remained relatively immune behind armour. In aggregate this created a weapon system of immense power and flexibility in operation, a power that was enhanced by the fitting of a No. 19 radio set in each fighting machine besides a few of the key administrative vehicles. Each No. 19 radio set performed three functions: its A set could send and receive speech up to 10 miles or morse up to 20 miles; its B set could do the same over much shorter ranges for intercommunication between individual tanks at troop level and it provided speech facilities for intercommunication between crew members. The infantry had radio sets of such poor performance that they had to depend upon conferences and personal contact between leaders and men for the dissemination of information and orders, whereas armoured soldiers could carry on a running dialogue just so long as they observed the essential disciplines made mandatory by the fact that only one set out of the 100 or more that might be found on an armoured corps radio net, could be used at a time. To neglect this discipline would 'jam' the whole network.

As a rule a battle lasts only a few hours, at the longest a week or more, but the time for preparation can be prolonged over years of training and rehearsal. A commanding officer, with the rank of lieutenant-colonel, had under him four majors in command of the three tank squadrons and the administrative Headquarters Squadron. Throughout the training period these officers and the junior leaders and men placed under them progressed by stages to a state of battle worthiness, a proficiency which was incomplete until consummated and proven by enemy fire

to the eventual performance of each tank's crew once it had been formed of commander, driver and co-driver, gunner and radio operator, whose other task was loading the turret main armament. No sooner had they been nominated as a crew than they began the next stage in learning, that of co-operation among themselves in making the tank a fighting unit which could make the best use of its strength and power. Simultaneously they learnt the art of sharing eating and sleeping arrangements often under conditions of discomfort in bad weather when heavily fatigued. Crew training would then merge with troop training. Next whole squadrons

The crew of a Valentine tank prepare a meal during an exercise in England in 1941. The men are members of the Royal Tank Regiment.

Right: An A13 Cruiser tank rams a bombed house during training in a blitzed area of London.

and the impact of fear. The officers acquired their basic training in tank duties — those of driving and maintenance, gunnery and radio — at recruit training regiments and in the Officer Cadet Training Units. At the latter would be taught minor tactics and how to command a troop in action. Their NCOs and men would also learn their basic skills at a training regiment and from courses held within their operational regiment, courses which, as time went by, would help select the men who would be the best sergeant and corporal tank commanders. The standard of individual training was, of course, fundamental

would manoeuvre together prior to taking part in regimental exercises during which, for the first time, the commanding officer saw his whole organisation at full stretch. Intermingled with this Collective Training would come live-firing exercises, ultimate tests in themselves of each crew's prowess and a clear indication from the record of hits on target as to a unit's initial fitness for battle. Compared with these exercises an armoured regiment's participation in major schemes involving complete brigades, divisions and corps was of less importance except as a test for commanders. But still the element of fear was

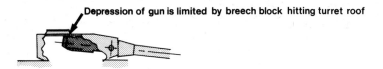
Depression of gun is limited by breech block hitting turret roof

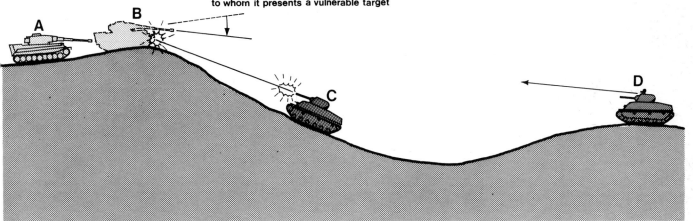

Tank in position B cannot depress gun low enough to engage tank at C
to whom it presents a vulnerable target

A   B   C   D

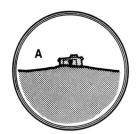

A

B

Tank A appears 'hull down' to observer in tank at D,   but fully exposed when it moves to position B in trying to
engage tank at C

Men of a German
PzKw 35(t) unit
are addressed by an
officer after the
Polish campaign.

A German anti-tank
gun passes two
knocked out
German tanks at the
approaches to a
French village in
May 1940.

British soldiers of the 8th Army cover a PzKw III J captured in North Africa. Note how the crew have loaded the tank with jerricans, spikes for adjusting the track links, a box on the rear decking and a string of water bottles along the stowage bin on the turret.

absent, the foe was only an umpire with a white flag, and not an armed and dangerous enemy.

In ideal circumstances (all too infrequently realised) an armoured regiment approached its first battle with crews from whom all the misfits had been removed and with equipment from which all the snags had been eliminated. Yet their first battle invariably produced major changes since only in battle could the deficiencies and omissions of peacetime training be discovered. The German panzer battalions which overwhelmed the British and French armies in May 1940 had been brought to a peak of efficiency in the campaign against Poland in September 1939, when various faults were noticed and eradicated. The

British armoured battalions which crushed the Italians in North Africa in the winter of 1940/41 did well as a result of earlier battles in the desert as well as the 1940 campaign in France. And so it was in every army which found itself thrust into war. Training was endless.

A Sherman Firefly
dug in hull down
on the German
border during the
severe winter of
1944-5. Hull down
a tank could see and
shoot the enemy,
but was often
invisible until it fired.

Advance to Contact

Only rarely did an armoured regiment go into battle on its own, since, when it did, disaster often occurred. Usually it was supported by artillery and accompanied by infantry and engineers whose task was to deal with opposition beyond the easy reach of tank weapons. When the tank commanding officer received his orders for an operation he was given far more information than the mere objective which he had to reach. He was told about the known or estimated enemy opposition which was to be expected and provided with intelligence describing the activities of flanking units or those which were to follow him into action and exploit such success as he won. He was also given a list of the units and sub-units allocated under his command or in support. Let us follow the procedures adopted by a British CO who had been allocated a battery of field artillery in direct support (meaning that the eight 25-pounder guns were for his exclusive use without being under command), a company of infantry and a section of engineers under command (meaning that they must implicitly obey his orders as if part of his own regiment) and ordered to attack a German outpost position prior to advancing as rapidly as possible against an enemy who had shown signs of preparing a withdrawal.

Having arrived at an outline plan based on a study of the map, the CO, if he had time, would reconnoitre the sector in the company of the battery and infantry company commanders. Together they would formulate a more detailed plan for dissemination to their sub-units — the CO to his squadron commanders and they to their troop leaders who instructed their tank commanders; the gunner to his troop commanders; and the infantry company commander to his platoon commanders who briefed their section leaders. Time was the controlling factor. With plenty to spare every level could indulge in careful discussion and study of the ground so that each man eventually knew the part he had to play: the less to spare, the scarcer became the briefing of the lowlier members in the team and the more that had to be passed over telephone and radio with a consequent loss of accuracy during dissemination. Moreover the use of telephones and radio gave rise to the danger of the enemy intercepting and understanding even coded messages. Indeed an increase in the number of radio sets under intensive use was a sign that an attack was impending. Furthermore, prior to an attack the extensive armoured regimental radio net had to be checked, resulting in a proliferation of tuning calls which not only identified the sort of unit using the air but, through cross bearings by direction finders, fixed locations in detail. Sometimes netting was done by reference to a master oscillator (called a wave meter) and sometimes with aerials detuned, but to be sure that all was working properly,

A T 34/76A. This early mark had a cast gun cradle, a single block driver's port, single horn periscope and unshielded hull machine gun mount. The first vehicles were completed in early 1940. Their low silhouette and 'short' 76.2-mm gun made them the most effective tanks of that period.

A Klementi Voroshilov Kv 1B. The KV 1B was distinguished from the KV 1A by its cast turret. It was armed with one 76.2-mm gun and three 7.62-mm machine guns, its 550 hp diesel engine gave a maximum road speed of 26 mph.

American tanks outside Chartres during a pause to check the vehicles and equipment after the capture of the town on 17 August 1944.

each set had to be made to respond to calls from the control station. Usually wireless silence was maintained to within an hour or so of the start time (called H hour) in the hope that, by then, the enemy would be aware too late to take effective counter measures.

The approach of an armoured regiment to its attack position was made by carefully scheduled stages governed by a well-established routine. From hidden concentration areas far behind the front (and therefore out of sight and beyond the perils of enemy artillery fire) the regiment would move by night into an Assembly Area that was perhaps some miles back or as close as 3,000 yards to the front line. In the Assembly Area, final adjustments to weapons and vehicles, and topping up with fuel after the approach march, took place while planning went on. The regiment might stay in this location for a

day or more, or perhaps just a few hours, but once the next move forward began to the Forming up Place (FUP), in ground just out of sight of the enemy, halts would be shorter and sometimes avoided altogether.

Infantry, travelling either in half-tracked armoured carriers or walking, joined the tanks in the FUP and there memorised tank recognition marks and finalised communication arrangements. In 1944 the infantry carried rather ineffective pack radios which failed more often than they succeeded in maintaining touch with tank radios. Sometimes they would talk to tank commanders through the telephone carried on the back of each tank, but as often as not the tank commander had either to climb down from his turret or the infantryman scramble up to talk to the commander. The whole business was haphazardly perilous because of the tank's tendency to attract enemy fire. And

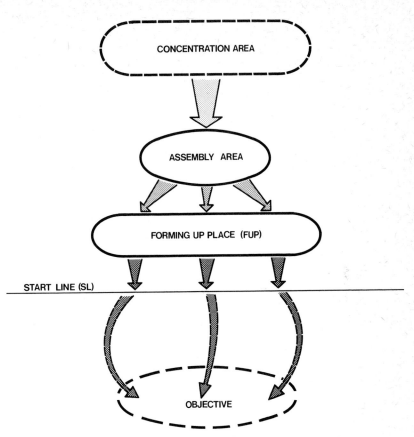

CONCENTRATION AREA

ASSEMBLY AREA

FORMING UP PLACE (FUP)

START LINE (SL)

OBJECTIVE

from this moment onward the danger of being hit by shell fire was omnipresent, for there was always the possibility of enemy artillery bringing down speculative fire on possible forming up places, picked from the map, in the hope of disrupting the beginning of an expected attack. Hence the selection of FUPs was a matter for inspired judgement. It was unwise to enter areas that were too obviously suitable for the purpose: on the other hand it was useless selecting a place that did not fulfil the demands of accessibility, that was too cramped or from which the exits were so poor as to prevent quick deployment to the next tactical bound — the start line (SL).

Whereas Assembly Areas and FUPs were of necessity physical features on the ground whose occupation in time was variable, the SLs were to some extent the opposite. They might be the line of a hedge or a stream but they could equally be a tape laid down

beforehand. Their purpose, however, was of crucial importance to the accurate launching of an attack. An attack was timed from the start line. When the first troops crossed it, that was H hour: anything which took place beforehand was called H minus and afterwards H plus. Phased movements and artillery fire tasks were geared to H hour. The easy identification of the SL was therefore its most important function since movement within a precise programme demanded accurate time keeping. And since troops had no need to stop on the SL it was not a necessity that it should be out of sight of the enemy, as was so essential with the Assembly Area and

The crew of a Sherman reload with 75-mm ammunition. They are passing the shells through the loader's hatch.

A *Panzerkampfwagen* 'Tiger' *Ausf E* model. The tank
had a green and brown camouflage over the
factory sand coloured finish. The Tiger had one
8.8-cm KwK 36 and two or three 7.92-mm MG 34
machine guns. Its Maybach engine developed
642 bhp at 3,000 rpm and gave a top speed on
roads of 23 mph.

A *Panzerkampfwagen* 'Panther' *Ausf A*. The tank was painted with a green on sand camouflage and treated with zimmerit anti-magnetic mine paste. The Panther was armed with one 7.5-cm gun and three 7.62-mm machine guns. It was powered by a Maybach HL230 P.30 with a maximum speed of 15 mph cross country and 34 mph on roads.

Above: Preparation for battle. Men of the 3rd The Kings Own Hussars clean the barrel of their Sherman tank.

Right: The driver of a Churchill tank greases the track bogies.

FUP. It had also to be aligned at 90° to the axis to impart correct direction.

A few minutes before the SL was crossed the overtures of battle were played. As the leading squadron of tanks, their guns loaded and hatches closed (except for that of the commander who otherwise might not have good all-round vision due to the lack of a cupola fitted with multi-periscopes) the opposing artillery began their exchanges. In support of the oncoming tank squadron, with a platoon of infantry in close attendance to the rear, the artillery opened with short, intensive concentrations of fire against known or suspected anti-tank gun positions. Reluctantly, perhaps, smoke would be laid across a threatened flank position, since to do so could sometimes be beneficial to the enemy. With tanks every bit as much as with infantry the governing tactical principle was that of movement accompanied by fire directed against the enemy — whether or not the fire was aimed as a means of deliberate destruction of a located target or scattered over an area. The arrival of high explosives and bullets in the vicinity of an enemy anti-tank gunner could shatter his composure and upset his aim even if it did not prevent him firing. Thus, in theory, and sometimes in practice, tanks advanced while dependent only upon fire from artillery. A time had to come, however, when the artillery ceased fire in order to avoid endangering friendly troops. But, in any case, artillery fire was not always sufficient to discourage the crews of enemy guns emplaced behind concrete or located in a defiladed position — above all guns mounted in tanks which were protected by armour plate which could move from one good fire position to another. Therefore every tank formation, be it a troop, a squadron or a regiment, endeavoured to provide its own close fire support in aid of its own movements

— and did so far more positively than the artillery because it usually engaged targets on direct line of sight.

Imagine the regiment's leading squadron advancing through a countryside mostly unspoilt by war in which trees, hedges and small hamlets intersect terrain which is gently rolling, featured by crests and a few vantage points of tactical importance. As shellfire falls on known or suspected German positions to the front, two tanks from each tank troop warily push their noses through the hedge which acts as a start line and speed up for the cover provided by the next hedge ahead. The remaining tanks to these troops expose only

A troop commander distributes rations to his men in a concentration area in France in 1944.

Left: A British soldier checks the ammunition of the .50 calibre machine gun mounted on his tank.

A Panzer IV/70 (Sd Kfz 162/1) often loosely known as a *Jagdpanzer IV*. This self propelled tank destroyer was painted in a spring camouflage scheme. It was armed with one 7.5-cm Stu. K42(L/70) with 55 rounds of HE and AP ammunition. Its Maybach engine gave a maximum road speed of 22 mph.

A Light Tank M3A1 "General Stuart", part of a
British reconnaissance detachment. The
Stuart or Honey was armed with one 37-mm M6
L/57 gun and three .30 calibre machine guns. Its
Continental model W670-9A petrol engine
gave a road speed of 36 mph.

their noses and turrets throught the hedge and spray the ground ahead with machine-gun fire hoping to shake the determination of bazookamen with their short-range, hollow-charge anti-tank weapons. Still farther to the rear the remaining two troops of the squadron (including one that contains Fireflies with the longer 17-pounder gun) keep watch along with the tanks of squadron headquarters, in hull down positions atop a crest some 400 yards behind the leading troops. Only their turrets and main armament are visible to the distant enemy. (This is the role, incidentally, in which the Russians and Germans preferred to employ their self-propelled guns though there were occasions when there was no option but also to put them in the lead).

The right flank troop in the lead has come close to its objective and is slightly ahead of its companion. At this moment a German anti-tank gun, concealed behind a bank in a small coppice to the flank, opens fire, penetrates the Sherman's armour and sets fire to the ammunition. Many things happen at once. Survivors among the crew struggle clear and run back the way they came, trying to tread in their tank's track marks since these are likely to be free of mines. The troop leader, commander of its companion tank, at once tells his driver to speed up left for cover and orders his

The crew of a German *Wespe* (Wasp) self-propelled 10.5-cm light field howitzer pose around their vehicle. The *Wespe* was a PzKw II chassis with the standard light howitzer, which had a range of about 13,400 yards.

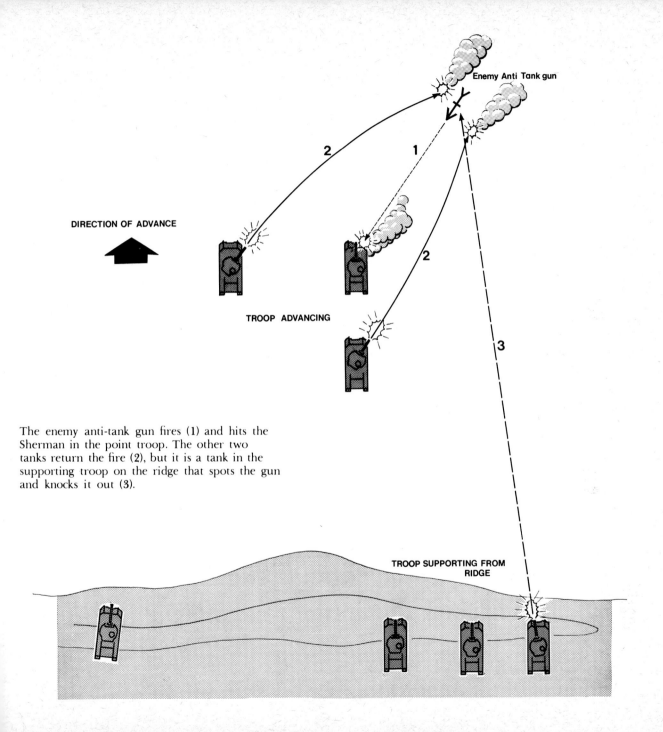

DIRECTION OF ADVANCE

Enemy Anti Tank gun

TROOP ADVANCING

The enemy anti-tank gun fires (1) and hits the Sherman in the point troop. The other two tanks return the fire (2), but it is a tank in the supporting troop on the ridge that spots the gun and knocks it out (3).

TROOP SUPPORTING FROM RIDGE

The Churchill AVRE with Small Box Girder Bridge.
The SBG could be positioned by a Churchill
manned by men of the Royal Engineers who
could operate from within the tank. It was one of
several bridge laying tanks developed
between 1943 and 1945.

The Churchill Crocodile had the standard six-pounder gun, but in place of the hull machine gun a flame gun was fitted and connected to a 6½ ton trailer containing 400 gallons of fuel, five pressure bottles and controls. The Crocodile had a maximum range of 360 feet. The fuel trailer could be jettisoned either when it had run out, or if it was hit.

Germany's tank killer. German soldiers manhandle an 8.8-cm Flak gun across a pontoon bridge in France in 1940. The '88' remained in service throughout the war.

gunner to traverse right and open fire on what he only guesses is the place where the enemy is located. Almost before the machine-gun has fired the driver, picking his own path, has driven headlong into a hollow just short of the hedge he was making for. Meanwhile the right flank tank of the left hand squadron has traversed right and fired two inch smoke bombs in the direction of the burning tank, first as cover against further enemy fire and also to help the crew to escape.

The classical counter anti-tank gun action by a troop was for one tank to engage the enemy by fire while the other (or others) manoeuvred, out of sight or under cover of smoke, for a position from which to destroy the enemy by fire or by charging and crushing the gun. In this instance the troop commander can see no way of dealing with the situation on his own. A move to the disengaged flank may expose him or his companion to unrevealed guns. In this case, however, there is no need for manoeuvre since one of the tanks on the high ground behind has spotted the anti-tank gun's flash. Its commander has ordered his gunner to traverse onto line, has estimated the range and given the order to fire a high explosive round which pitches short of the target but on line. The gunner is told to go up half a turn on his elevating wheel and the next round falls beyond. 'Down a quarter turn', and the 'bracket' is filled when the third round falls right onto the enemy gun.

The advance continues until the leading troops come closer to higher ground 1,500 yards distant when artillery and then mortar fire begins to fall among them, causing only superficial damage but forcing each commander to crouch low in his cupola and thus becoming deprived of full vision. Anti-tank fire comes from three points across a frontage of 1,500 yards. One flash seems to be from a German tank that is fleetingly seen to drive into a hull-down position before retiring from view. Mounting caution grips each British tank commander and those in the lead seek cover from which to search the ground ahead. Radioed contact and sighting reports begin to come back from the leading tanks and, since at this moment the entire regiment is on the same radio frequency, can be monitored by all commanders who mark the results on their maps. A section of two Stuart light tanks, reconnoitring cautiously along the exposed right flank, catch a particularly rewarding sight of the enemy tank reversing to a fresh fire position and of an anti-tank gun hidden from view in a re-entrant. The leading squadron commander with his artillery Forward Observation Officer (FOO, who also travels in a tank of his own) begin to assemble a picture of a German platoon or company location barring the way. The FOO begins to range his guns onto the targets that have been located while the squadron commander assesses the best way of defeating this tough opposition.

He reasons that a direct assault would be far too costly but that the mere survival of the reconnaissance tanks to his right gives hope that this is the safest approach for an attack on the German left flank. His plan, like the best of their kind, is simple. It is to hold the enemy attention by fire from the leading troops which have gone to cover in the front row, to bombard located enemy positions with artillery while moving his own headquarters along with the two relatively disengaged supporting

A German 8.1-cm mortar crew in action on the Aisne in France in 1940. As one man prepares to load a bomb the other crew members steady the bipod legs.

A Sherman Crab Mark I. This type of mine clearing tank was known widely as a 'Flail', and it would explode the mines buried in its path. At the rear of the tank was a box containing powdered chalk which was used to mark the cleared lane.

A Sherman Firefly with crudely applied winter camouflage in the winter of 1944-5. The Firefly was a Sherman re-armed by the British with a more powerful 17-pounder gun in place of the 75-mm gun. About 600 Fireflies were ready for the Normandy campaign and played a vital part in actions against Tigers and Panthers.

troops along the right-hand approach. Meanwhile the Regimental commander places the whole company of half-track mounted infantry at the squadron commander's disposal, warns a second squadron to be ready to exploit any success that the leading squadron might achieve. He then drives forward in his tank to watch the attack developing.

The Germans too are observing closely and it is not long before they detect the move against their left flank. This they had expected and to counter it have in rear, a Mark IV and a Panther tank which now shift to previously decided positions to deal with the oncoming threat. A tank versus tank action is thus in the offing but not to the Germans' immediate advantage as in an ambush. For the pilot of a light reconnaissance British Auster monoplane, seeking targets for the guns, spots the German tanks advancing and radios a warning through the artillery net for relay to the tank regiment. Reading from his map, the squadron commander appreciates that a slight diversion of one troop should position it nicely to engage the enemy before they have arrived in a threatening locality. Radio orders

go out, the troop divert and arrive at a copse just in time to detect the German Mark IV at about 700 yards. At this range he knows that he can penetrate the German armour at almost any point, though it is better for his gunner to avoid aiming at the thick frontal plate. In fact the Mark IV is at an angle. Firing from the halt, his first shot, spotted by a red tracer flare, throws up earth just to the front of the target. The German begins to turn for cover, but his opponent has marked the fall of solid shot, adjusted his aim up half a target with slight 'lead' for movement — and sent his next shot straight through the side armour into the fighting compartment where the ammunition explodes killing the crew. At this moment the Panther comes into sight and halts, fully exposed to view, at 800 yards.

The victorious British troop leader has now been joined by his troop sergeant's tank and together, in trepidation, they face a more formidable opponent with only the Panther's frontal armout to shoot at. The first shot comes from the troop sergeant and strikes the Panther's glacis plate to rebound high in the air. The Panther fires and the shot from its

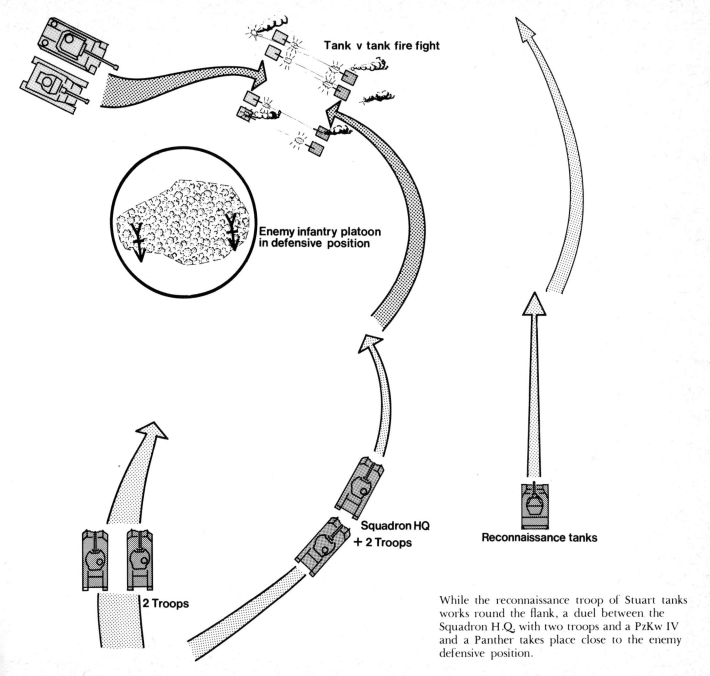

Tank v tank fire fight

Enemy infantry platoon in defensive position

Squadron HQ + 2 Troops

2 Troops

Reconnaissance tanks

While the reconnaissance troop of Stuart tanks works round the flank, a duel between the Squadron H.Q. with two troops and a PzKw IV and a Panther takes place close to the enemy defensive position.

45

long 75mm gun, with a velocity of 3,068 feet per second compared with 2,050 of the British 75mm gun, sheers through the turret mantlet of the British troop leader's tank, kills commander and gunner and buries itself in the radio set. The three survivors struggle to safety but are chopped down by a nearby German infantry machine-gunner. The British troop sergeant fires a second forlorn shot and orders his driver to reverse, but again the shot bounces off the Panther and he is too late in taking evasive action as the Panther also picks off his tank with a well conducted piece of gunnery. Unseen by the Panther commander, however, the troop corporal has swung still further right, out of sight along a gully — overrunning in the process a solitary German outpost. He manages to find his way into position, unobserved, at 600 yards to the Panter's flank just as it is beginning to retreat to cover. At this range the much thinner side armour of the German tank cannot withstand the British 75mm gun and now it is the German's turn for destruction.

At a price the British squadron has fought its way to the flank of the German locality and, in swopping pieces with his enemy has achieved a decisive superiority in both numbers, position and weight of metal. Already one of the German anti-tank guns has been destroyed by artillery fire and the rearguard commander, whose instructions were purely to impose delay on the British, orders withdrawal.

Now is the time for the British regimental commander to press his advantage with a quick, determined pursuit, but he is denied immediate information of the German intention. The one tank which can actually see the Germans pulling out is that of the victorious troop corporal, but his attempts to pass the information by radio are frustrated since the impact of firing his gun has knocked the 19 set off tune. Nobody hears his repeated

calls until the radio operator, tense with anxiety, is reminded to check net and put matters right. By then the Germans are in full flight and the CO can conduct only a belated pursuit. A fresh squadron is thrown into the lead while the one that has seen action pauses for reorganisation.

The appearance of the German tanks and the sight of their burning victims has a distinctly cautionary effect upon the pursuing British. Well aware that every topographical feature may hide an ambush and that in a stand up fight the Germans can out-range them, the leading troops advance with circumspection and have to be urged on constantly by their commanders — for the divisional commander is harrying the brigadier, the brigadier chasing the regimental commander, the CO his squadron commanders and the latter are doing all in their power by personal example to encourage their tank commanders. Typical of the sort of delay which minor enemy resistance causes, occurs when a single German *Panzerjäger* IV opens fire on the leading tank of the Advanced Guard and knocks off its idling wheel. Seeking a flanking position the troop leader's tank

detonates a mine which breaks a track. Contact reports from the leading tank send shivers down everybody's spine by announcing, erroneously, that there is a Tiger to their front. The squadron commander tries to manoeuvre the Firefly troop to advantage but a single shot from the *Panzerjäger* deters that scheme and a map reading error misdirects another of his troops. Bereft of a weapon to out-match the enemy he must look elsewhere for salvation. If he had a troop or battery of medium 5.5 inch guns in support he would have called upon these to shell the 'Tiger' and drive it out, for it had been discovered that these 80lb shells distinctly rattled the German crews whose top armour was unequal to a hit should one, by chance, be obtained. Lacking medium guns he calls for air support and half-an-hour later four Typhoon fighters armed with rockets circle overhead while an RAF officer in a nearby tank describes the target's location to them. One by one the Typhoons peal off and dive to launch their rockets. None hit (the chances of these unballistic missiles doing so was less than 1%) but the *Panzerjäger* commander considers that he has achieved all the delay that is possible and so reverses out

47

Above: An 8.8-cm Pak 43/3 L/71 *auf Panzerjager* Sd Kfz 173, generally known as a *Jagdpanther*. This was the ideal SP anti-tank gun with a low silhouette, and a maximum speed of 28 mph.

Far Right: Tanks of the 14th Armoured Division of the U.S. 7th Army knocked out in a narrow street in Lohr, in Germany. The tank in the foreground has extemporised armour made from sand bags.

of the hiding place to race away to the next ambush position. He has held up the advance for well over an hour and induced further caution in the enemy, besides inflicting minor losses.

By phased withdrawals from place to place and defile to defile, the Germans back into their next main line of resistance. Tanks and self-propelled guns in withdrawal were invaluable since they had the ability to 'hide, shoot and scoot' with the minimum likelihood of being caught. Discovery of their hides before they can fire was essential for the attackers, but light tanks, armoured or scout cars were just as likely to be ambushed as any other vehicle, while infantry patrols in the lead on their feet took too long and were prey to *any* kind of weapon. Spotting aircraft might sometimes penetrate the enemy's camouflage, but more often than not a machine and men had to be sacrificed in return for discovery of the enemy's presence. Of course, if a gap in the enemy screening line was found then the ambushers themselves could be taken in rear and ambushed, but then again it would be armoured vehicles that were of most value for the defenders whose chances of last minute escape would be improved by armoured mobility.

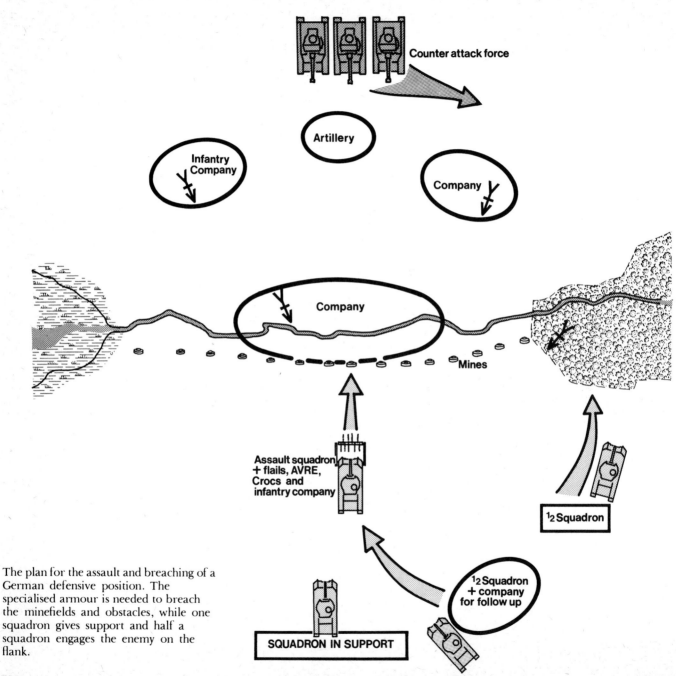

Counter attack force

Artillery

Infantry Company

Company

Company

Mines

Assault squadron + flails, AVRE, Crocs and infantry company

¹₂ Squadron

¹₂ Squadron + company for follow up

SQUADRON IN SUPPORT

The plan for the assault and breaching of a German defensive position. The specialised armour is needed to breach the minefields and obstacles, while one squadron gives support and half a squadron engages the enemy on the flank.

Assault and Breaching Operations

The defensive deployment which the Germans are adopting is orthodox as governed by their own rules. Infantry platoons and companies are interlocked on dominating ground overlooking an obstacle — in this case a stream with soft ground adjacent and mines blocking those places where the soil is firm. Within each company locality are to found anti-tank guns dug in while the field artillery area also has an anti-tank role. To enhance security the battalion has been allocated three *Panzerjägers* to provide a local but mobile defence, one hidden in a house, one in a hollow covered by shrubs and a third dug into a hole which has been scooped by the engineers. And since this position occupies vital ground which the Germans wish to hold for at least three days, a combat team of three Tigers and a reinforced company of infantry has been stationed 3,000 yards to the rear for a counter-attack when required.

Intelligence of this major position with all the preparation, such as digging, placement of weapons and supplies, is extremely difficult to conceal and the advancing British will have long been aware of it from air reconnaissance and agents' reports. So greater caution is prevalent as the defended ground comes into sight. All at once it becomes clear that an ambush sprung against a tank of the Reconnaissance troop is, in fact, actuated by the outer defences. Artillery fire begins to fall among the leading troops and British artillery retorts with concentrations upon a farm house that commands the main road that is also the divisional centre line. The squadron commander appreciates that this is an objective that will have to be cleared by infantry and, as commander of the Advanced Guard, he makes a joint plan with the infantry company, (if the country had been close, above all forest or jungle, it is more likely that the Infantry Commander would have made the plan) and the artillery battery commander. Their scheme simply complies with the demands of fire and movement. While the field artillery brings down a preliminary concentration upon the farm, the tank squadron deploys to give flank protection and allocates two troops to work in close conjunction with the infantry. Meanwhile the infantry half-tracks disgorge their men in dead ground some 800 yards from the farm. At H hour the assault infantry and tanks advance, the artillery gives two minutes intensive fire upon the objective and then switches to lay smoke over commanding ground ahead while the rest of the squadron fires random shots into nearby places where the enemy might be. At the same time the regimental commander has brought a second squadron forward in an attempt to swing round the right flank and maintain momentum as well as being a measure of distraction.

German defensive fire from mortars crashes down but without avail since the infantry have

Above: A German N.C.O. demonstrates the Panzerfaust 30 one man anti-tank weapon. It had 3½ lbs of explosive in the war head and could penetrate 200 mm of armour.

Right: An MG34 machine gun team in action in France in 1940.

been carried beyond the planned zone of the German concentration and the tanks are not in the least inconvenienced. The leading platoon of infantry gets to within 50 yards of the farm house and is joined by a troop of tanks whose machine-guns are rattling almost continuously. A German bazooka man inadvisably tries to take a shot and is mown down by an alert infantry machine-gunner. A German machine-gunner who unleashes a burst from a flank position is spotted and blasted by two tanks whose commanders have been waiting for something like that. The assault goes in and there is stern work with bombs and sub-machine-guns amid the smoking farm's ruins. Meanwhile the tanks advance beyond and cut off an escaping enemy while drawing fire from the next German position close to the stream upon which the defence is based. Indeed the battle has now become general as the farm outpost is secured. Artillery and anti-tank fire from the Germans leave no doubt that they intend to stay and that their strength is such that a prepared

British assault will be required for their removal.

The defensive position is laid out to withstand every possible kind of assault and is economically sited to compel their opponents to regroup — in effect to cause prolonged delay, while upsetting the rhythm of the advance. Self-supporting company localities made doubly secure by minefields (anti-personnel as well as anti-tank) are laid between two major topographical features — a lake on the right and thick woods on the left. Anti-tank guns are dug-in among each company and backed up by the artillery area with all guns sited, primarily, to cover the minefields and the stream which runs through the frontal companies. The *Panzerjäger* IVs are also to be found dug-in among the reserve infantry to rearward, ready to move forward or

to a flank to hold off enemy tanks at long range or deal with a sudden incursion, probably as part of a local counter-attack force. The stream, 20 feet wide, acts as an anti-tank obstacle whose strongest sector is near the lake where the ground is softest on either bank. And to the rear, in hiding amid woods, lie the 3 Tigers and company of infantry.

Rapidly the British discover the extent of these defences. Aerial photos tell part of the story and are rapidly supplemented by exploration. For the squadron which tries to force its way past on the right near the woods meets a blaze of fire from a few German anti-tank guns and the crescendo of gun-fire from behind the stream leaves no doubt that this area will have either to be fought over or left until formations, working ahead some miles away to the right, have broken through and levered the Germans out of this place. But such leverage will take time to apply, the corps commander is pressing for faster progress and the divisional commander is energetically prodding the brigade commander who appreciates that the leading armoured regiment is no longer suitable on its own for the task. In any case the road has to be opened up to supply any further advance

An M8 armoured car stopped while its American crew watch the effects of shell fire on a French village in 1944.

Flail tanks of the 3rd Battalion The Scots Guards carry men of the 2nd Bn. The Argyll and Sutherland Highlanders during operations in north-west Europe in 1944.

in depth since it is destined to become a main supply route. It is time for the armoured orchestra to be augmented. Regrouping takes place on the British side while reconnaissance continues, and the intelligence picture is built up. A battalion of lorried infantry is called forward, the artillery is reinforced to that of a full regiment plus a battery of medium 5.5 inch guns, and specialised armoured units — Sherman flails for clearing mines, Churchill AVREs to help cross the stream and Churchill Crocodile flame-throwing tanks to cow the enemy infantry, are added. The attack is to be direct, a formal breaching operation — similar in outline to that employed at Cambrai in 1917 but much more sophisticated in technique and in the use of specialised AFVs to enable engineers to work from behind armour.

The routine assembly of attacking forces continues apace, for the need to resume the advance at the earliest possible moment is paramount — part and parcel, in fact, of all armoured operations in which speed must be of the essence in order to throw the enemy off

balance. In this case it is impossible, however, to be ready before dusk and the divisional and brigade commanders consider that, such is the complex nature of the German position, it would be inadvisable to commit men and machines to a quickly arranged night attack with hardly any time for reconnaissance. Confusion in unknown ground might well have fatal consequences and, in any case, tanks which lacked night vision telescopes, could not fire their guns accurately in the dark. So a conventional dawn attack is adopted in the hope that, at half light, the enemy will shoot badly and that, if all goes well, maximum daylight hours will be available for exploitation and the fullest benefit extracted from overwhelming Allied air power. Of critical importance in deciding the hour of attack is the light available: there must be sufficient for tank gunners to see the graticules in their telescopes so that they can aim straight, a condition known as 'first telescope light'. Nevertheless, the preliminary bombardment can begin a few minutes before,

Tanks of the 9th R.T.R. with men of the 6th Royal Scots Fusiliers advance through a smoke screen during fighting near Tilly in Normandy on 26 June 1944.

should it be felt desirable, though it is more likely that in the preceding hours the artillery will concentrate on countering enemy gun batteries.

The British infantry battalion commander decides to lead with one out of his three companies to seize the German positions holding that part of the stream and minefield through which it is intended to make the breach. A troop of flail tanks will beat their way to the edge of the stream, exploding mines as they go, and will be followed by an AVRE bearing a Small Box Girder Bridge to be dropped across the stream as the battle proceeds around them. Then the flails will cross the bridge and continue to flail a lane through the minefield while remaining infantry companies pass through to assault the German companies beyond. Artillery and mortar concentrations will fall on known enemy locations, particularly those suspected of concealing anti-tank guns. The task of the armoured regiment will be to subdue, by direct gunfire, if not by its mere presence, those opposing elements which try to interfere with the breaching operation. In this phase their main preoccupation is direct help to the specialised armour, for when a flail is flailing it kicks up clouds of dust or mud and its crew cannot see or manoeuvre for their own protection. The

Two 15-cm heavy infantry howitzers on SP mountings prepare to give supporting fire during fighting around Carroceta in February 1944. Also visible are two knocked out Allied Shermans and a half-track carrying the ammunition for the SP guns.

CO of the armoured regiment commits his entire unit to the attack, allocating one squadron to direct support of the breaching operation and the remainder to lend fire support from hull down positions in rear against the main enemy position and the edge of the woods to the right. But the squadron on the right is only partially involved since, when the time is ripe, it will be pulled back and fed through the breach to take the lead in exploitation of success. In this exploitation phase it is to combine with a company of infantry in the attack on the main German defended locality, an operation which will involve a troop of Crocodile flame-throwers whose need for close armoured support for demands of defensibility is as urgent as that of the flails. Therefore the tank squadron commander witholds two of his troops to link up with the infantry and Crocodiles prior to the assault so that they can plan detailed and close co-operation during the assault.

Yet, although the orchestration of the on-coming performance in battle is arranged to the fullest extent, it is an event of the greatest rarity when even a well founded operational plan proceeds to perfection. There are so many things — human and mechanical — to go wrong and every effort of the enemy is geared to bring disruption and failure. On this

Russian engineers with Teller 43 anti-tank mines which they have lifted from a German minefield. The man in the foreground is unscrewing the pressure plates on two mines to make them safe.

A Sherman flail tank
crosses the River
Orne in Normandy
over a Bailey Bridge.
Note the spare
chains for the flail
drum stored in a rack
on the side of the
tank.

A Churchill AVRE
named Scimitar
tows a sledge
loaded with fascine
bundles, while
another follows
with a fascine bundle
attached to the
hull front. Fascines
were intended for
filling in anti-tank
trenches. The
AVRE was a tank
designed for
special engineer
tasks.

occasion the relative simplicity of the initial breaching operation is its own guarantee of success, particularly since the minefield is both shallow and the mines are not fitted with delayed action fuses, timed to go off under the flails. So the path is cleared to the stream's bank, the flails peal off to right and left and the AVRE trundles forward, nose heavy with its SBG bridge extended, and drops its load in the correct place — though dangerously tilted to one side. Meanwhile the German reaction accumulates from early ripples of defensive fire on the FUP to plunging outbursts along the crossing places. German machine-gun fire is almost non-existent, however, since the presence of tanks in the assault wave deters them and the tanks are unmolested because the German anti-tank guns have either been destroyed by artillery, or shot up by tank guns or withold their fire for a propitious moment

Above: Churchill tanks give British soldiers a lift near St Pierre Torentaine.

Left: Men of the United States 46th Armoured Infantry Battalion of the 5th Armoured Division ride in their White half-track "Copenhagen" The half-track was a vital part of any tank infantry unit because it provided protection and mobility to infantry.

59

when they can shoot unobserved. The German infantry outposts are overwhelmed and a British bridgehead formed. Casualties have been light and mainly the result of mortar and shell-fire. The leading tanks begin to cross the SBG bridge, but cautiously due to its tilt. The schedule begins to fall behind time. Meanwhile a second troop of flails is told to open up a second lane so that another crossing place can be formed.

At this the Germans react more forcefully. Two *Panzerjägers* creep from cover to engage the British tanks crossing the bridge, constantly shifting position after firing in the hope of imparting an impression of greater strength and also to throw off the fire of British tank

Top Right: Refilling a Churchill Crocodile fuel trailer. The thick sticky flame thrower fuel could be projected 360 feet.

Right: Men of the 2nd Derbyshire Yeomanry take cover during a tank infantry attack. In the background are the smoke and flames of a Crocodile tank.

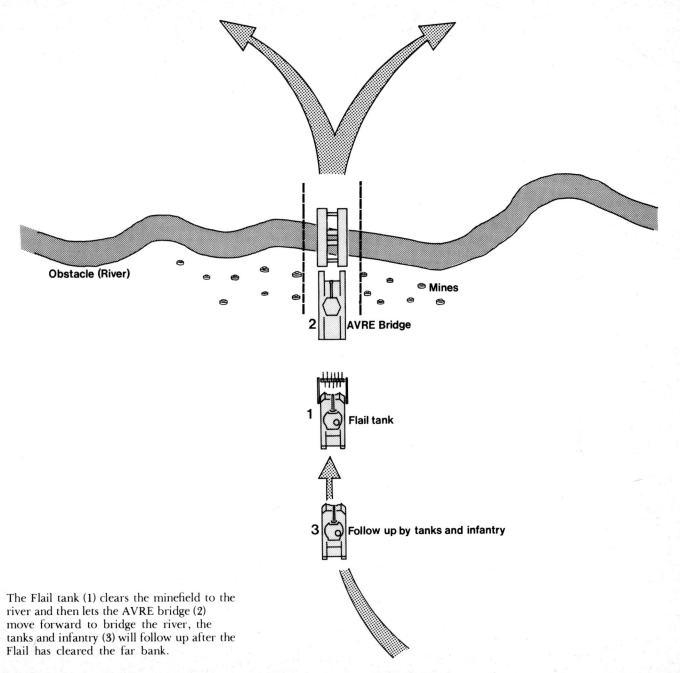

Obstacle (River)

Mines

2 AVRE Bridge

1 Flail tank

3 Follow up by tanks and infantry

The Flail tank (1) clears the minefield to the river and then lets the AVRE bridge (2) move forward to bridge the river, the tanks and infantry (3) will follow up after the Flail has cleared the far bank.

A German machine gunner in action with his MG 34 during fighting in France in 1940. The MG 34 fired at 800 to 900 rounds per minute and had an effective range of about 800 yards.

gunners. They kill one flail and damage another just after it has crossed the bridge. There is a hold-up since the infantry will not advance without the tanks and the tanks are reluctant to cross until the mines have been cleared. But the lone flail already across has pounded ahead for 20 yards without detonating a mine, so the squadron commander, while directing his rearward troops in sniping at the *Panzerjägers,* sternly orders his leading troops over the bridge. Close by his commanding officer watches with approval, calculating the moment when the second wave — the infantry company with its Crocodiles — should be launched.

Visibility is now becoming obscured by dust and smoke generated in volume. Each tank commander, like every infantryman, begins to feel cut-off. Anxious calls over the radio, while presenting a fairly clear picture to the squadron and regimental commanders, provide a source of worry to lower mortals. Every gun that fires in opposition is reported as an 88 — though none of these are in evidence among the German armoury here, the biggest anti-tank gun being a 75mm, and most only 50mm. Likewise the *Panzerjäger* IVs are reported as Panthers or Tigers. It is now that the steadying voices of the higher commanders over the radio become of paramount

importance in maintaining morale as well as the direction of the original plan.

Caught in crossfire the leading infantry company goes to ground, and when the next wave is sent through it too flags but a few yards further on. But the three Crocodiles, dragging their trailers, are crossing the bridge — all that is except the last. The slope on the bridge, which has been increasing, causes its trailer to slip sideways and then the whole edifice cants over. The lane is blocked and the attack must go ahead only with what has got

across — two companies of infantry, two surviving flails, two Sherman gun tanks and two Crocodiles, not one of which mounts a gun any bigger than 75mm calibre. They gather themselves while the tanks on the home bank are deployed to give maximum gunfire in support, and the Crocodiles begin to climb the slope towards their objective, a platoon of infantry in attendance according to plan. The nearby Shermans and flails lay down machine-gun and high explosive fire ahead and to the flank, effectually deterring German short

Above Left: British troops training in England practise obstacle crossing. The soldier is carrying a Bren gun, the section LMG.

Above: Panther tanks in Russia.

range anti-tank weapons and knocking out an anti-tank gun. Meanwhile the *Panzerjägers,* in unwisely climbing to the top of the crest in order to shoot down the slope at the Crocodiles, have exposed themselves to a flurry of shot from every British tank in sight. They burn on the ridge.

German reinforcements are arriving, however. The Tigers are coming, spotted and rocketted by four RAF Typhoons, but unchecked in the drive to the crest line. They are too late to save their infantry, for the leading Crocodile has already loosed off a high flame shot out of range and disheartened several

Germans. And as the Crocodiles get closer and pump flame and smoke in a flat trajectory at the infantry earthworks, their occupants depart — a few in flight, the majority with hands raised for captivity. There is nothing so terrifying as fire — and that applies to tank crews as well. Quick to follow the success of the flame attack, the British infantry run up to secure prisoners and consolidate the captured position on the crest line. A few minutes later the Tigers arrive.

One is unlucky. A British PIAT operator spots it at once and throws a bomb which penetrates the side armour and sets the heavy

A PIAT (Projector Infantry Anti-Tank) team in the ruins of Caen in 1944.

tank alight. But the other Tigers, seeing their comrade's fate are more cautious and take care not to expose themselves to the British infantry nearby as they intently bully the British armour. There begins a battle of giants in which the Tigers systematically seek out the British armour at longer range on the other side of the stream. A gun duel at 1,500 yards

American soldiers
shelter around a
camouflaged
Sherman during
fighting in France.

German Tiger tanks
in the Brenner
pass. The crews
have used their tent
sections to make
shelters by their
tanks. There are dust
covers over the
guns.

A French crewed Sherman knocked out during fighting in the Saverne Gap. A shot has passed straight through the turret.

opens with the advantage firmly on the German side. For at that range not even the 17 pounders can penetrate the Tigers' frontal armour whereas the German 88 gun can easily cut through the armour of the Shermans. Picking their shots with mounting enthusiasm, the German gunners hit, destroy and drive off every visible British tank at long range and then edge slightly forward to shoot the Crocodiles, flails and Shermans which are vainly seeking shelter in shallow hollows or behind hedgerows. One Sherman goes part of the way to redressing the balance by manoeuvring to a flank and killing a Tiger before it is itself shot by a German bazooka man at 20 yards range. Meanwhile the British medium guns are being used to shell the remaining Tiger which is forced to withdraw when a shell lands on and penetrates its top engine deck, causing damage that demands

British 5.5-inch gun
howitzers. The
"55" could fire a
100-lb shell 16,000
yards or a 80-lb
shell 18,500 yards.
The plunging fire
from these guns
could penetrate the
thinner armour of
the top plates of
tanks like the Tiger
or Panther.

American M3 light tanks move through a shell damaged French town. The M3 was known as the "Honey" by the British and the "Stuart" by the Americans.

instant repair. In any case it has almost exhausted its armour piercing ammunition and has to move back to replenish.

The Tiger's departure is timely for the British since it enables the flails and AVREs to open a second gap to complete their task successfully and for the next squadron of tanks, with the remaining infantry, to cross and continue the assault on the main German

position. Now it is the British armour which dominates, simply because of a numerical superiority and not from anything like the technical advantage in armour which the Tigers had clearly demonstrated. Working closely, the combat team of tanks and infantry clear the remainder of the opposition to the crest and prepare to continue the advance — in fear of that single Tiger which lurks ahead.

A disabled Sherman
is passed by
another Sherman
during the advance
in France in
August 1944. These
tanks were mass
produced in the
United States and
their sheer numbers
dominated the
battlefield.

An American soldier
fires the .50
calibre machine
gun on his Sherman
during the fight
for a bridge over
the Marne in 1944.

An M10 Tank
destroyer on
guard during the
American invasion of
southern France.

The battle continues as a segment of the mosaic of engagements covering a battle front that is in almost perpetual motion — as one mechanised force impinges upon another and struggles for a local supremacy which can be expanded to encompass a vast frontage and, ultimately, the entire campaign. But the governing struggle for supremacy, based upon the destruction of armour before major progress can be made, has been defined in the clash described above. In head on combat a numerically superior force has defeated its technically superior opponent. Attrition has been employed but an attrition very different from that involving the infantry masses and their artillery helpers in 1917. For such was the rate of attrition in the 1940s that it was often impossible to secure a ruptured front with sufficient reinforcements before the condition of mobile war overwhelmed the survivors. Thus tanks and armoured vehicles dictated the mode of campaigning and though the machines and weapons are now much more deadly, the lessons taught then still apply in the 1970s.